National Museums Scotland

The Covenanters

Claire Watts

SCOTTIES SERIES EDITORS
Frances and Gordon Jarvie

Contents

First edition published in 2011
by NMS Enterprises Limited – Publishing
a division of NMS Enterprises Limited
National Museums Scotland
Chambers Street, Edinburgh EH1 1JF

Text © Claire Watts 2011
(for image and further ©, see below and page
viii of the Facts and activities section)

ISBN: 978–1–905267–38–5

Book design concept by Redpath.
Cover design by Mark Blackadder.
Layout by NMS Enterprises Limited – Publishing.
Printed and bound in the United Kingdom by Bell
& Bain Limited, Glasgow.

CREDITS

*Thanks are due to the following individuals and
organisations who supplied images and photo-
graphs for this publication. Every attempt has
been made to contact copyright holders to use the
material in this publication. If any image has been
inadvertently missed, please contact the publisher.*

COVER ILLUSTRATION
SCOTTISH NATIONAL PORTRAIT GALLERY
A Section from Processional Frieze in the Central
Hall of the Scottish National Portrait Gallery by
William Hole (including: Charles I; Alexander
Leslie, Earl of Leven; Archibald Campbell, 8th Earl
of Argyll; James Graham, 5th Earl of Montrose;
Charles II and James VII).

NATIONAL MUSEUMS SCOTLAND
(© National Museums Scotland)
for pages 10 (stool); 15 (Glasgow Cathedral);
17 (flag); 19 (scene from *Cloud of Witnesses*);
20 (powder horn); 22 (pendant); 25 (execution
scene from *Daniel Wilson's Scrapbook*); 26 (plug
bayonet); 27 (Peden's mask); 33 (Cameronian
Regiment); 35 (The 'Maiden'); 38 (National
Covenant) – Facts and activities section, page 1
(Conventicle); vi (D).

SEALED KNOT SOCIETY
With thanks to the above for kind permission to
reproduce images of battle re-enactments.

FURTHER CREDITS (see p. viii of Facts and
activities section).

SCOTTIE BOOKS

For a full listing of NMS Enterprises Limited –
Publishing titles and related merchandise:
www.nms.ac.uk/books

Timeline of events

This timeline provides a summary of some of the main events shown in this book. Page numbers in brackets beside each entry will tell you where to find more information about each event.

Year	Events in Scotland	Events in England	Events in Britain
1625	Act of Revocation (page 8)	❖	After the death of James VI of Scotland and I of England, his son Charles I comes to the throne (p. 8)
1633	Charles I visits Scotland for his coronation (p. 9)	❖	
1637	Riots against new prayer book (p. 10)	❖	❖
1638	National Covenant signed (p. 13) Glasgow Assembly held (pp. 14–15)	❖	❖
1639	First Bishops' War (pp. 16–17)	❖	
1640	Second Bishops' War (p. 17)	❖	
1641	Charles I visits Scotland (p. 9 and 17)	❖	
1642	❖	English Civil War breaks out (p. 18)	
1644	Montrose becomes Commander of Royalist forces in Scotland (p. 20)	Battle of Marston Moor (p. 18)	
1645	❖	Battle of Naseby (p. 20)	
1646	❖	Charles I surrenders to Covenanters (p. 18)	

Year	Events in Scotland	Events in England	Events in Britain
1648	Whiggamore Raid (p. 19)	Battle of Preston (p. 19)	❖
1648–50	'Rule of the Saints' (p. 19)	❖	❖
1649	Scots declare Charles II as King (p. 22)	English Commonwealth (p. 22)	Execution of Charles I (p. 22)
1650	Cromwell invades Scotland (p. 22)	❖	❖
1651	Charles II crowned King of Scotland (p. 23)	Battle of Worcester (p. 23) Charles II defeated and flees to mainland Europe	❖
1658	❖		Cromwell dies (p. 24)
1660	❖	Charles II restored to the throne of England (p. 24)	❖
1666	Pentland Rising (pp. 28–29)	❖	❖
1669	Government introduces 'Indulgences' to bring outed ministers to Kirk (p. 30)	❖	❖
1679	Assassination of Archbishop Sharp (p. 30) Battles of Drumclog and Bothwell Brig (p. 31)	❖	❖
1681	Test Act (p. 32)	❖	❖
1685	'The Killing Time' (p. 34)	❖	Charles II dies. James VII of Scotland and II of England is crowned King (p. 34)
1687	4th Declaration of Indulgence grants freedom of worship	❖	
1688	James VII and II escapes to France (p. 36)	William of Orange marches on London (p. 36)	The Glorious Revolution. William III and Mary II come to power (p. 36)
1689	James VII and II deposed	❖	
1690	**Act of Parliament re-establishes the Presbyterian Church of Scotland (p. 37)**		❖

Who were the Covenanters?

… and what was the cause they were prepared to die for?

All over Scotland, but particularly in the south-west, stone monuments commemorate those who were killed during the 17th century because they were **Covenanters**.

The Covenanters were a group of people in Scotland involved in a struggle between their religious beliefs and their allegiance to the King in London. The resulting conflict lasted for at least 50 years from 1638 when protesters first signed the document known as the **National Covenant** (see page 12), setting out their aims. The end came in 1690 when the recently crowned King William of Orange established a new Church of Scotland considered acceptable to most of the Covenanters. The upheaval spread not just over Scotland, but played a part in civil conflict in England and Ireland as well.

Over the 50 years, the Covenanting move-ment changed. It started as a campaign of peaceful protest but quickly grew to become a civil war. Covenanters played an important role in the English Civil War (1642–1651) and even controlled the government of Scotland for a few short years. When this government

The Monument to the Wigtown Martyrs, at Wigtown, was erected to commemorate two women who were drowned for refusing to deny their Covenanting beliefs (see page 35).

collapsed, the Covenanters were persecuted by the King and forced to become a secret movement. The Covenanters, commemorated in the stone memorials across Scotland, were victims of the harsh and generally unjust actions of the authorities trying to crush what they saw as a radical and dangerous political group.

Many people remember the Covenanters as freedom fighters, struggling against oppression so they could follow their own beliefs and way of life. Some would argue that they were determined to impose their views on others. Their political achievement was to create a national government in Scotland which was not answerable to the English Parliament. As such they became a symbol of Scotland's national identity.

What were they fighting for?

During the 16th century, Protestantism spread throughout Europe in a movement known as the **Reformation**. Protestants believed that the Catholic Church was outdated and they were looking for a new, simpler way to worship.

The Reformation reached Scotland in the 1550s, led by a Scottish clergyman, John Knox. At first there were simply sermons and books and pamphlets, spreading the new ideas. Before long there were riots and destructive attacks on Catholic churches and monasteries. Finally there was outright rebellion against the French Catholic leadership of Mary of Guise, the regent who ruled Scotland in place of her daughter, Mary, Queen of Scots. When Mary of Guise died in 1560, the Scottish Parliament rejected the Pope's authority, forbade the celebration of the Catholic Mass and approved a Protestant Confession of Faith. Thus when Mary, Queen of Scots arrived in Scotland to take up her throne in 1561, she found herself ruler of a Protestant country. John Knox admonished Mary for supporting Catholic practices and openly called for her execution when she was later imprisoned for her alleged role in the murder of her husband, Lord Darnley.

Eighty years later, when the Scottish people found their Church threatened by the monarchy, they were prepared to fight for it again – this time as Covenanters.

Find out more about the Church of Scotland on pages 6 and 7.

The Martyrs' Memorial

In the crowded graveyard of Edinburgh's Greyfriars Kirk stands an impressive memorial. It was built in 1706 to commemorate the 18,000 people, including the Marquis of Argyll in 1661 and James Renwick in 1668, who were executed or lost their lives for the Covenanting cause.

Religion in the 17th century

Today, most people consider religion to be a matter of individual choice, but things were very different in 17th-century Scotland.

Since the Reformation of the 16th century, the majority of churches in Scotland and England had been **Protestant**. The main church in Scotland – the **Reformed Church of Scotland** – was set up as a **Presbyterian** church. Presbyterian **Protestants** believed that the country's government should not be in charge of the church, that all ministers should be equal, that bishops should not rule over them, and that the monarch should not be the head of the church.

England's main church, the Church of England, was ruled by bishops appointed by the King who was the supreme head of the Church. Churches ruled by bishops in this way are called **Episcopalian**. In addition, the **Church of England** had retained many of the practices of **Roman Catholicism**, which Presbyterians considered to be wrong.

After ascending the English throne in 1603, King James VI of Scotland and I of England restored the powers of bishops over the

James VI & I

James VI of Scotland (1566–1625) became James I of England in 1603 on the death of Queen Elizabeth I.

Scottish Church. By his death in 1625, the Church of Scotland was an unhappy mix of part-Presbyterian and part-Episcopalian.

Going to church

Everyone was expected to attend church services every Sunday. Members of the **kirk session** known as **searchers** would roam the streets looking for those who were not in church. The morning service would last from eight or nine o'clock until eleven or twelve. Then, after a break for something to eat, people would return to church until around four in the afternoon.

Other religious groups had to worship privately in their own homes. Roman Catholics were particularly feared and even despised, and there were severe laws against practising Roman Catholicism. These laws, however, were rarely enforced at this time.

The Church of Scotland
in the 17th century

COURT: Kirk Session

Members:
People who attend local church.
A teaching elder and ruling elders.

Area:
The parish.

Duties:
Help the minister look after the parish.

Run the school and look after the elderly.

Keep law and order.

Approve the appointment of the minister put forward by the local laird.

COURT: Presbytery

Members:
Ministers from a small area.
A teaching elder and ruling elders.

Area:
Several parishes.

Duties: Matters that the individual kirk sessions could not handle themselves.

COURT: Synod

Members:
A selection of the ministers from each presbytery and chosen elders.

Area:
Region covered by several presbyteries.

Duties: Matters concerning the entire region. (A bishop was at times in charge of each synod.)

COURT: General Assembly of the Church of Scotland

Members:
Ministers from all parts of the country and chosen elders.

Area:
All of Scotland.

Duties: Matters that affected the whole country. The General Assembly could only meet if the King summoned it.

A King's interference

When Charles I came to the throne in 1625, he began to make changes to the way that Scotland was ruled, but he did not consider asking the Scots what *they* wanted.

From the very first, Charles made enemies amongst the English and Scottish nobility. His **Act of Revocation** in 1625 threatened to take back vast areas of church land that had been given to the nobility after the Reformation. In the end, the Act was hardly implemented, but the nobility remained suspicious of the King.

Landowners were also angry that Charles was demanding taxes from them far more often. In the past they had only paid out in times of war, but now taxes were gathered every year.

Charles ruled Scotland through a body called the **Scottish Privy Council**, made up of important men of the realm. However, the King never sought the Privy Council's advice, but simply gave orders which he expected them to obey. He also appointed several bishops to the Privy Council. This annoyed

William Laud

Archbishop of Canterbury

Although people called the new prayer book 'Laud's liturgy' after William Laud (1573–1645), it was actually written by Laud and King Charles in consultation with the Scottish bishops, and contained many parts of the old Scottish prayer book. However, Laud soon became the focus for protesters' anger and was eventually beheaded in 1645.

the nobility because they believed that they alone should run the country, without any interference from the Church.

But what aroused the fury of even more Scots was Charles's meddling with the Kirk, without consulting the General Assembly. Although in fact born in Scotland, Charles had grown up in England and loved the Anglican church. Charles wanted the Church of Scotland to be more like the Church of England, and he forced Anglican **liturgy** on the Kirk. He began by making changes to the way services were performed, stating that the communion table should be placed at the far wall of the church rather than in the middle. He also instructed ministers to wear short white smocks called **surplices** in a similar fashion to English clergymen; and he introduced kneeling at communion.

In 1633, Charles finally visited Edinburgh to be crowned King of Scotland. During his stay he decided that St Giles, the High Kirk of Edinburgh, would become a cathedral.

In 1637 it was announced that the King had commanded the preparation of a new prayer book. *The Book of Common Prayer* was to be used in all church services. Despite rumblings of opposition, Charles, as usual, did not consult the Scottish Parliament or the General Assembly. He declared that any resistance to the new prayer book – known more commonly as **'Laud's liturgy'** – would be considered treason.

All across Scotland, a movement against the King's religious reforms began to grow.

Charles I

Charles I (1600–1649) believed in **Divine Right**. This was the idea that a King was granted his position by God, and no person had the right to question his actions, but should simply obey his orders. He also believed that, as King, he was the **Supreme Head of the Church**, not just in England, but in Scotland too. In fact, Charles was not a frequent visitor to Scotland. He came only twice – for his coronation on 18 June 1633 and to try to drum up support against the English Parliament in 1641.

Why do you think Charles I introduced the new prayer book?

Answer on page 40

Riot at St Giles

There was talk about the new prayer book all over Scotland. Should the King tell people how to worship? Was Charles trying to turn the Kirk into part of the Church of England? Might the reforms lead to the return of Catholicism?

Tradition has it that the woman who threw the first stool was Jenny Geddes, a local vegetable seller. However, her name was not mentioned in accounts of the events until much later, so it was probably made up to make the story more dramatic. The picture (above) shows the kind of stool that might have been thrown. It bears the date of 1565.

The first reading of the new prayer book was set to take place in Edinburgh on Sunday 23 July 1637. All the important people of Edinburgh were inside **St Giles' Cathedral** that day, but a crowd had gathered outside. The moment the Dean began to read from the prayer book, shouts broke out around the church. As the Bishop of Edinburgh climbed into the pulpit to try to restore order, a woman stood up, picked up the wooden stool she had been sitting on and threw it towards the Dean and the Bishop. The congregation joined in, sending a hail of prayer books, bibles and stools flying towards the front of the church.

The church was cleared of protesters and the doors were locked while the service continued inside. Outside, the crowd could be heard, banging on the doors and shouting.

Sticks and stools also flew in St Andrews, and in other churches around Scotland, as congregations reacted angrily to the first readings of the new prayer book.

Elsewhere in Edinburgh the story was the same. The minister of Greyfriars had to flee from his church, chased by an angry mob of shouting women. In the Trinity Kirk, the minister heard the news of the events in the other churches, and decided to stick to the old prayer book. But, all over Scotland, riots broke out whenever the new liturgy was introduced.

Although it was said at the time that the St Giles riot and all the other violent outbursts happened spontaneously because of ordinary people's disgust at the new prayer book, it is more likely that this was a carefully planned campaign by ministers and possibly some of the nobility.

St Giles' Cathedral

Seal of St Giles

St Giles' Cathedral (see interior on the left), also known as the **High Kirk of Edinburgh**, stands on the Royal Mile between Edinburgh Castle and the Palace of Holyrood House.

The church was founded in the 1120s. By the middle of the 17th century, it had become a large building with many adjoining chapels paid for by craftsmen's guilds, nobles and rich merchants.

Although referred to as a cathedral, it was only the seat of a bishop from the years 1635 to 1638 and 1661 to 1689.

Visit St Giles and see how many references to the Covenanters you can find.

The National Covenant

Alexander Henderson

Furious about the opposition to his prayer book, Charles insisted that the Privy Council made sure that the book was used.

But the Privy Council did nothing at all. This was in part because they were afraid to act without consulting Charles, and because sending messages to and from the King based in London took many weeks.

However, some of the members of the Privy Council were secretly on the side of the agitators. They too did not want bishops in the Privy Council.

Hundreds of nobles, lairds, ministers and burgesses of the town began to gather in Edinburgh, bringing petitions signed by more and more people. They elected a group of representatives to urge the King to remove the bishops from the Privy Council and to withdraw the new liturgy. Since the Privy Council was doing nothing to restore order, this group – called '**The Tables**' – soon became an alternative government in Scotland.

> As minister for Leuchars in Fife, Alexander Henderson (*c*.1583–1646) opposed the introduction of the new prayer book. The clarity and vehemence of his opposition made him an obvious candidate to help draw up the Covenant.

The Tables chose a clergyman, Alexander Henderson, and a lawyer, Archibald Johnston of Warriston, to write a document to unite all the people opposed to Charles's highly unpopular policies. It was also designed to clarify their aims. This document became known as the **National Covenant**.

What the National Covenant says …

The National Covenant was written very carefully indeed so that it did not appear revolutionary. It referred back to legal agreements and Acts of Parliament made by Charles I's father, James VI and I, which promised to uphold both the Presbyterian Church and the laws of Scotland. It then rejected what it called 'innovations' or new policies in religion and government that had been introduced by Charles. The document emphasised that those who signed it remained loyal to the King.

A popular tale of the time was that many of those who signed the National Covenant did so with their own blood!

A united rebellion

'Whatsoever shall be done to the least of us for that cause, shall be taken as done to us all, and to every one of us in particular.'

This quote from the National Covenant shows that the people who signed were doing more than just expressing their own personal grievances. They were promising to join together in a movement that would involve each individual in supporting and defending all the others in pursuit of their common cause.

Why do you think the authors of the National Covenant were careful not to sound too revolutionary?

Answer on page 40

The signing of the Covenant

On 28 February 1638, nobles and lairds gathered at Greyfriars Kirk, Edinburgh, to sign the Covenant. The following day ministers and representatives of the burghs and towns added their names. Copies of the Covenant were then taken all over the country for people to sign.

Many saw this as rededicating themselves to God, and were proud to do so, but there were also many who were pressured into signing. The Covenant was keenly received in southern Scotland, but in Aberdeenshire, Banffshire and the Highlands it did not prove so popular.

The Glasgow Assembly

At last King Charles began to recognise the serious threat to his authority.

In the summer of 1638 he agreed that both a **General Assembly** and **Parliament** could be held in Scotland. But secretly Charles was playing for time while he tried to raise an army to invade the country.

It is not easy to assemble an army in secret, however, so news of the King's preparations soon reached the Covenanters. It was clear now that negotiating with Charles was pointless. He could not be trusted.

The Covenanters made sure the General Assembly would be packed with their supporters. Although it was supposed to be a Church assembly, noblemen got themselves elected as elders of the Kirk so they could attend. Meanwhile, elders and ministers from north-east Scotland, who were likely to support the King were excluded. So were all the bishops.

The Assembly began in **Glasgow Cathedral** on 21 November 1638. It had been 20 years since the last General Assembly, so the first days were filled with discussion about how

Archibald Campbell

8th Earl of Argyll

When the Marquis of Hamilton stormed out, Archibald Campbell (1607–1661), the Earl of Argyll, showed his support for the Covenanters for the first time. Campbell was the most powerful man in Scotland, ruling over a vast area and able to call on an army of 5000 men. He was a member of the Privy Council and had not yet signed the Covenant, but he was soon to become one of the most influential leaders of the Covenanters.

the meeting should be conducted. As soon as the business of the Assembly began, heated arguments broke out. The King's representative, the Marquis of Hamilton, found himself unable to control the meeting, so on 28 November he declared the Assembly dissolved, and then he walked out.

Since the King's representative had dissolved the Assembly, it was now deemed illegal. However, the members continued to sit for another three weeks. During that time they abolished episcopacy from the Kirk and all the acts of past General Assemblies which allowed the King to order the Kirk to do his bidding.

Glasgow Cathedral

Sir Walter Scott's book *Rob Roy* gives an account of Glasgow Cathedral which is also known as the **High Kirk of Glasgow** or **St Kentigern's** or **St Mungo's** Cathedral.

Built before the Reformation, from the late 12th century onwards, it is thought to be located where St Mungo, the patron saint of Glasgow, built his church. St Mungo's tomb is in the lower crypt. The building is no longer technically a cathedral as it has not been the seat of a bishop since 1690.

Choosing a venue

Glasgow was a small town in 1638, with a population of around 5000 folk. Why do you think the James Hamilton, Marquis of Hamilton (below), chose to summon the General Assembly in Glasgow instead of in the capital, Edinburgh?

Answer on page 40

They also condemned the new prayer book as unlawful, since the Kirk had not agreed to it. They excommunicated all the bishops, and abolished the role of bishop. They then declared that, in the future, the General Assembly would meet every year. And on that final note, the Assembly of 1638 dissolved itself on 20 December.

Fast fact

One of the charges that the Covenanters brought against the bishops was that they played cards on a Sunday!

The Wars of the Covenant

Although the Covenant had promised to support the King, Charles was getting ready to attack Scotland. It was a time of unrest that would last more than ten years.

The first clashes of the Wars of the Covenant were known as the **Bishops' Wars**. Charles planned to attack Edinburgh while his generals invaded by sea and Royalist clans sympathetic to the King attacked from the Highlands. But in March 1639, the Covenanters seized ports to prevent troop landings, and took control of strongholds such as Edinburgh Castle.

Alexander Leslie
Earl of Leven

The commander of the Covenanter army was Alexander Leslie (c.1580–1661). He had spent most of his life fighting abroad, rising to the rank of field marshal in the army of the King of Sweden. After leading the Covenanters to victory in the Bishops' Wars, Charles I made Leslie the Earl of Leven in 1641, hoping to gain his support.

Covenanter Army

The Scottish army was highly motivated. The soldiers were fighting for a cause they believed in. They were also well fed and regularly paid. Many trained professional soldiers who had been fighting in other countries returned home to join the Covenanter army. In contrast, the English army was poorly paid, badly trained and most were not convinced they were fighting for a just cause.

Covenanter flag

The Garscube Flag, reputedly carried by Colonel Stewart of Garscube at the Battle of Worcester in 1651 and then used again at the Battle of Bothwell Brig (see page 31).

Over the years, the writing has faded, but can you decipher the words on the flag?

Answer on page 40

The King's army advanced to Berwick on 30 May, and on 5 June the Covenanter army made camp at Duns Law, 18 kilometres from Berwick. Although Charles's army was bigger, the Covenanter army was better trained, disciplined and commanded. The King hastily negotiated a truce and the **First Bishops' War** was over.

Charles agreed to another General Assembly and a meeting of the Scottish Parliament, and the decisions of the Glasgow Assembly of November 1638 were ratified. But this was another challenge to the King's authority and Charles began to raise funds to gather his troops once again.

In May 1640, while the King sat in London, the Covenanters struck first, occupying Aberdeen and invading the lands of the Royalist clans in the Highlands. The port of Dumbarton was besieged to prevent the King's army landing there.

By August, the Covenanter army of around 20,000 men had massed on the English border. On the 20th they marched into England, bound for Newcastle. After a brief skirmish at Newburn, the English army withdrew and the Covenanters marched unopposed all the way into Newcastle by the end of the month. Once again, Charles was forced to agree to a truce. The **Second Bishops' War** had lasted just ten days.

After the Second Bishops' War, the Covenanter army remained in the north of England until a permanent settlement was negotiated in the summer of 1641. As part of the deal, the King was made to pay the Scots £850 per day to cover the costs of billeting the army in England until they returned home.

The Solemn League and Covenant

The Covenanters had won … but only for a short time.

Charles had been forced to accept the decisions made by the General Assembly and the Scottish Parliament. But in 1642, civil war broke out between the King and the English Parliament. Scotland was soon drawn into the conflict.

The King was fighting for his right to rule England the way he believed a king should, while Parliament wanted to reduce his power, as in Scotland. If Charles won, it seemed very likely that he would undo all the decisions recently forced upon him in Scotland.

An agreement known as the **Solemn League and Covenant** was drawn up between the Covenanters and the English Parliament. A Covenanter army would support the Parliamentarians against the King in their civil war, and in return the English Parliament promised to promote the Presbyterian religion throughout England and Ireland.

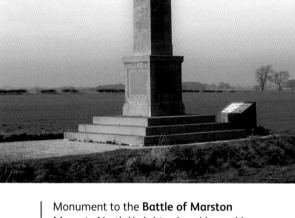

Monument to the **Battle of Marston Moor**, in North Yorkshire. Local legend has it that Cromwell directed his army from behind the clump of trees on the horizon.

In July 1644 the Covenanters helped the Parliamentarians to win a massive victory at the Battle of Marston Moor. Defeat swiftly followed defeat for Charles, and in 1646 he surrendered to the Covenanters.

From 1646–1647 the King was held captive at Anderson Place, known as the Newe House, in Newcastle, under the guard of the Earl of Leven. It was here that Charles was finally given over to the English Parliamentary commissioners.

For an entire year, the Covenanters held Charles at Anderson Place in Newcastle, demanding that he sign the Covenant. The King obstinately refused and the Covenanters returned to Scotland, handing him over to the Parliamentarians. As a result, the English Parliament backed out of the deal with the Covenanters and rifts started to appear within the movement.

Charles was now imprisoned on the Isle of Wight and once again he turned to the Scots for help. There were still some nobles who supported him, hoping to protect Presbyterianism. Most Covenanters, however, would not help him because he would not sign the Covenant, but royalist sympathisers among the Covenanters made an alliance with Charles, known as the **Engagement**.

With most of the Covenanter army refusing to fight for the King, the **Engagers** raised a new army. However, the recruits were badly led and poorly equipped and no match for the English Parliamentary forces' **New Model Army** led by Oliver Cromwell. At the Battle of Preston in August 1648, 2000 Scottish soldiers were killed and 8000 captured.

After the defeat at Preston, 2000 fervent Covenanters, known as the **'Whiggamores'** marched from south-west Scotland towards Edinburgh, occupying the capital in their protest against the Engagement.

With the support of Cromwell and his army, Archibald Campbell, the Earl of Argyll (see page 14), along with the most extreme of the Covenanters, seized control of the government of Scotland. The **Treaty of Stirling** was signed on 27 September 1648; that effectively ended the Engagers' dominance and their supporters slipped away into exile.

A new regime, known as the **Kirk Party**, set about building a godly society, based on Presbyterianism and the Covenant.

'The Rule of the Saints'

The years from 1648 to 1650 when the country was governed by the Kirk Party are known as **'The Rule of the Saints'**. During these years, all the 'ungodly' were removed from positions of power and from the army. Fierce punishments were meted out to anyone who failed to go to church or was suspected of witchcraft or immoral behaviour, including torture and death.

The Great Montrose

One of the first nobles to sign the National Covenant in 1637 was James Graham, Earl of Montrose.

James Graham
5th Earl of Montrose

James Graham (1612–1650) was made a marquis by the King in 1644. He was a brilliant military leader, defeating enemies of greater numbers with a mixture of skilful tactics and sheer daring. To the end he protested that he was a real Covenanter as well as a Royalist.

But Montrose was also convinced that Scotland needed a king. So while the Covenanters, led by Argyll and Leslie, were busy fighting against Charles in the civil war in England, Montrose led a Royalist army on Scottish soil.

Montrose had served in the Covenanter army that invaded England in 1640, but he wanted to curb the King's power, not get rid of him. Alarmed at the extremism of Argyll and his followers, Montrose secretly offered to help Charles. And so, in 1644, when the Covenanters invaded England, Charles gave Montrose command of Royalist forces in Scotland. However, with only his Graham clansmen to fight for him, Montrose had little support among those in power. The Kirk had denounced him as a traitor to the Covenant and Royalists distrusted him as a turncoat, even jailing him for a short time in 1641.

Montrose gathered an army of Highlanders and 2000 Irishmen fuelled by their hatred of the Campbells. Within a year this army had won a series of brutal and brilliant victories at Tippermuir, Aberdeen, Dundee, Inverlochy, Auldearn, Alford and Kilsyth, and Montrose now controlled the north of Scotland. After Charles's defeat at Naseby, Montrose made his way south to join the King in England. But as he travelled south, the Irishmen and Highlanders drifted back to their homes or to other battles. Few Lowlanders joined Montrose in their place.

Montrose's remaining forces were then defeated at Philiphaugh, near Selkirk, by

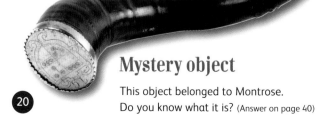

Mystery object

This object belonged to Montrose. Do you know what it is? (Answer on page 40)

the Covenanting army newly returned from England. Montrose himself fled to Europe.

In 1650 Montrose returned to Scotland with 1200 men from Germany, Denmark and the Orkney Islands, ready to fight for the recently crowned Charles II. But while waiting for reinforcements, his army was defeated at Carbisdale, and he was forced to flee again.

After four days of wandering wounded through the countryside, Montrose finally surrendered to Neil McLeod of Assynt, who promptly betrayed him. He was brought to Edinburgh a prisoner and on 20 May, without trial, Montrose was sentenced to death. The next day he was paraded through the streets of Edinburgh before being hanged at the Mercat Cross. Hung, drawn and quartered, his head was placed on a spike outside the Edinburgh Tolbooth and his limbs sent to Glasgow, Perth, Stirling and Aberdeen. In 1661 he was finally laid to rest in St Giles' Cathedral.

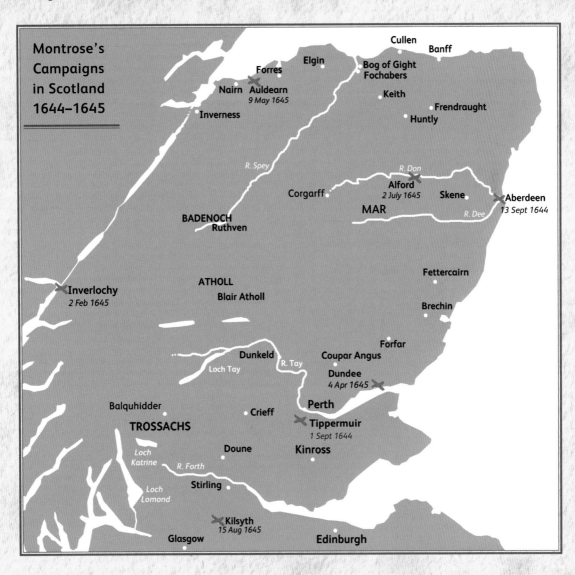

Montrose's Campaigns in Scotland 1644–1645

Cullen
Banff
Elgin
Forres
Bog of Gight
Fochabers
Nairn Auldearn
9 May 1645
Keith
Frendraught
Inverness
Huntly
R. Spey
R. Don
Corgarff
Alford
2 July 1645
Skene
Aberdeen
13 Sept 1644
MAR
R. Dee
BADENOCH
Ruthven
Fettercairn
ATHOLL
Inverlochy
2 Feb 1645
Blair Atholl
Brechin
Forfar
Dunkeld
Coupar Angus
Loch Tay
R. Tay
Dundee
4 Apr 1645
Balquhidder
Crieff
Perth
TROSSACHS
Tippermuir
1 Sept 1644
Doune
Kinross
Loch Katrine
R. Forth
Stirling
Loch Lomond
Kilsyth
15 Aug 1645
Glasgow
Edinburgh

Oliver Cromwell

By January 1649 the Parliament in England had executed Charles I and abolished the monarchy. England now became a republic, known as the **Commonwealth**.

A heart-shaped gold and enamelled pendant, dated *c.*1650, containing a miniature painting of Charles I, a lock of his hair, and part of the blood-stained shirt he wore at his execution.

Charles I, however, had not just been King of England but King of Scotland too, and the Scots were not ready to do without a king. A week after the execution, Charles I's son, also called Charles, exiled in Europe, was proclaimed King by the Scottish Parliament.

The English Parliament could not stand by while Scotland supported a new king and in July 1650 an English army led by Oliver Cromwell invaded Scotland.

At first the Scots pushed Cromwell's army back to Dunbar, but when the Kirk Party insisted that all non-Covenanters were removed from the army, including most of the professional soldiers, the Scots were no longer a match for the well-trained English. Nonetheless, the Church, which was funding the Scots, insisted they continue to fight.

The Battle of Dunbar lasted just two hours. The English lost just 30 men while around 3000 Scots were killed and 10,000 taken prisoner. Cromwell quickly took control of most of southern Scotland.

Oliver Cromwell

Oliver Cromwell (1599–1658) was a member of the English Parliament. He was unhappy with the way Charles I was running the country. He was responsible for making the New Model Army into a superbly trained fighting force.

'Stoope, Cha[...]
II having [...]
was for[...]
the su[...]

Charle[...] [...]ing of
Scot[...] [...]June,
C[...] [...]o fight the
[...]tirling in
[...]ell defeated the
[...]en marched on
[...]y, however, was to
[...]England open for the

[...]harles took the bait. As Cromwell captured
[...] Charles's army marched into England,
[...]outh-west and hoping to pick up
[...] the way. But few joined him,
[...]harles reached Worcester
[...]0 men.

[...]sued Charles, gathering a force
[...]men. He blocked off the routes
[...]London and Scotland, then forced
[...]cottish Royalists back inside the walls of
[...]orcester. On 3 September 1651 a vicious
battle raged through the streets, with most
of the Scottish leaders captured or killed.
Charles fled to Europe.

After the defeat at Worcester, Cromwell
abolished the Scottish Parliament and
made Scotland part of the Commonwealth.
Scotland would now be occupied by an
English army until 1660.

[...]les II

[...]es II (1630–1685) was determined to win
[...]ck his father's throne, but the Kirk Party
insisted that he could not become king until he
signed the Covenant. Charles detested their
stern, gloomy brand of religious fanaticism, but
when Montrose failed to regain the throne by
force, the young Charles gave in and signed both
Covenants.

Remind yourself what Scotland was like when
Charles II arrived there. Look back at the box on
'The Rule of the Saints' on page 19.

The outing of ministers

For seven years Oliver Cromwell ruled the Commonwealth under the title 'Lord Protector', until his death in 1658.

The political crisis that followed his death led to Charles II being restored to the throne in 1660. The English army that had been occupying Scotland returned to London.

A mood of celebration took hold throughout Britain. Everyone wanted to put the turmoil of the past 20 years behind them. Charles II went a step further and cancelled every act that the Scottish Parliament had passed between 1640 and 1649, including the one that made the Kirk Presbyterian.

The powers that the Scottish Parliament had gained were removed, so that Scotland would once more be ruled by the King from London. The Covenants themselves were declared illegal, and many surviving copies were burnt in public. It was as though the Covenanters had never existed.

The Kirk too returned to the way it had been before Charles I's time. Charles appointed new bishops. Services were conducted in the

Archibald Johnston
Lord Warriston

Archibald Johnston, Lord Warriston (1611–1663), was a lawyer, one of the authors of the National Covenant, and a firm Covenanter and a leading member of the Kirk Party (see page 19). After the **Restoration** of Charles II in 1660, he fled to Europe, but was captured and brought back to Scotland to face punishment (see opposite).

old ways, before the introduction of the new prayer book which had sparked off the Covenanter struggle. Lastly, all ministers would again have to be approved by the local laird, and they must declare an oath of allegiance to the bishops and the King.

Though many people were happy to accept the changes, the last two changes were too much for many ministers. They believed that laymen should not have authority over the Kirk. About a third of all ministers, 262 in total, refused to agree and were thrown out of their parishes and forbidden to preach.

Rumbles of discontent began in parishes that had lost their ministers, mainly in the south-west of Scotland. People disliked the inexperienced young ministers who replaced the outed ministers. Some began to refuse to attend Kirk services. Another rebellion was growing.

A King's retribution

Charles II had both the Earl of Argyll and Archibald Johnston of Warriston executed for treason because they had helped to govern the country under Cromwell.

Johnston met his fate by the hangman's noose, while Argyll died at the hands of 'the sweetest maiden I ever kissed' – Edinburgh's beheading machine (see page 35).

Withdrawing the troops

When the 10,000-strong occupying English army left Scottish soil, the barracks and forts they had used at Leith, Ayr, Perth, Inverness and Inverlochy were pulled down or put to other uses.

A detail of a map of Perth (below) shows the outline of the fort. This was Cromwell's fort, known as 'The Citadel'.

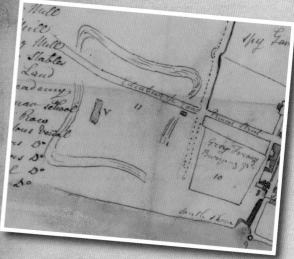

Ayr Fort has now been mostly dismantled, with various artefacts placed around the town. This gun, outside the walls of the fort, is a medium field weapon typical of the period of the Cromwellian citadel at Ayr.

Conventicles

The Covenant was now a thing of the past for most people …

However, for the outed ministers and many of their parishioners, the Covenant was more than a document. It was a promise that they had made to God and they could not abandon it just because the government said it was illegal.

These unwavering Covenanters could not accept the new Kirk, with its bishops and the King at its head. For them, Jesus was the head of the Kirk, and no human being could take this position. Having a person at the head of the Kirk was considered too close to Catholicism.

Some of the outed ministers took to preaching to these Covenanters in private houses, farm buildings or out among the hills. These gatherings, or **conventicles**, were illegal, so news of them had to be spread secretly. The ministers were not supposed to come within twenty miles of their former parishes, let alone preach. They lived as outlaws, constantly on the run from the authorities.

Alexander Peden
known as Prophet Peden

Prophet Peden (1626–1686) was one of the most famous of all the outlawed preachers. A former minister of New Luce in Galloway, Peden wandered the countryside gathering huge crowds of faithful Covenanters, sometimes having to make daring – and narrow – escapes from the authorities.

The first conventicles were small assemblies, but gradually they grew larger and larger, some with as many as 10,000 people. The authorities were determined to stamp out these rebellious gatherings. People who refused to go to services at the Kirk were fined.

A plug bayonet with a wooden hilt that was said to have belonged to Alexander Peden. The bayonet slid directly into the barrel of a musket. This, however, prevented the gun from being able to fire.

Soldiers were sent to scour the countryside for conventicles. They watched for small groups of people disappearing off into the hills, then followed their trail, listening out for the sounds of a preacher or singing.

The Covenanters, however, were ready for many attacks, and as the troops fell upon a conventicle, worshippers scattered. The soldiers chased the fleeing Covenanters and captured as many as they could. People attending conventicles began to arm themselves, ready to fight back.

Mystery object

Do you know what this curious object is? And how it is connected to **Prophet Peden**?

Answer on page 40

Below: Sir George Harvey's painting *The Covenanters' Preaching* (c.1830), depicts a conventicle during the 17th century in Scotland. On a desolate Scottish hillside a group of Covenanters meet to listen to their preacher. Afraid of persecution by Charles II's army they meet in secret. Most of the men carry arms in case of an ambush.

The Pentland Rising

Sir Thomas Dalyell

General Tam Dalyell (*c.*1599–1685) was a fervent Royalist who fought for Charles I until his defeat at Worcester in 1651. Dalyell then fled to Russia where he served and trained Tsar Alexei Mikhailovitch's army. Dalyell returned home in 1660, and the newly restored king, Charles II, made Dalyell commander-in-chief of his forces in Scotland.

Many people in south-west Scotland still remained loyal to the Covenants, and in November 1666 growing discontent sparked some new troubles …

Fines for not attending kirk, harsh treatment by soldiers, and high taxes, sparked a serious, though short-lived, Covenanter uprising. On 13 November 1666, a mob of around fifty armed farmers entered Dumfries, where they captured James Turner, the commander of the region's troops. The rebels declared loyalty to the King and the Covenants, then set off to march to Edinburgh to lay their grievances before the King. As they marched, their numbers swelled to over 1000.

The rebels expected to gather more supporters as they approached the city, but instead their numbers began to dwindle. Differences of opinion and the cold, wet weather made many turn for home.

A people's rebellion

The 1638 National Covenant was originally known as the **'Noblemen's Covenant'**. The nobility had been the leaders of the Covenant movement at the beginning. By 1666, however, they were happy with the state of the country and considered the Covenant to be a thing of the past. The Covenanters who took part in the Pentland Rising were ordinary folk, attempting to make themselves heard by those in power.

When the Privy Council heard that a mob was approaching the city, they were convinced this was the start of a major rebellion. As the rebels neared Edinburgh, cannons from Edinburgh Castle were wheeled to the city's gates. The rebels retreated into the Pentland Hills to decide what to do next. They were not prepared for battle. Most were armed with pitchforks and sticks and few had horses.

General Tam Dalyell and his troops had been tracking the rebels all the way from south-west Scotland. The soldiers attacked as the rebels camped for the night at Rullion Green. The rebels put up a brave fight, but they were no match for the trained soldiers. Fifty Covenanters died and 80 were taken prisoner. Although the uprising had caused very little harm, the Privy Council decided to make an example of the prisoners, hoping to crush any future rebellious ideas. Two were tortured to discover who the ring-leaders were, then 36 rebels, including those on the memorial below, were hanged at the Mercat Cross in Edinburgh. Some were dismembered and pieces shown in the Covenanters' own locality as a warning. The remaining prisoners were transported to colonies in America or the West Indies.

The words on the memorial below say:

Stay, passenger take notice what thou reads!
At Edinburgh lie our bodies, here lie our heads;
Our right hands stood at Lanark, these we want.
Because with them we share the Covenant.

Memorial to the Battle of Rullion Green (above) and a memorial (right) at Hamilton Parish Church to four men executed in Edinburgh in 1666.

Murder and rebellion

James Sharp

Archbishop of St Andrews

James Sharp (1618–1679), had been a leading Covenanter, but became a supporter of the restoration of the monarchy and the return of bishops to the Church of Scotland. Charles II made him Archbishop of St Andrews in 1661.

Scotland's government did not know how to deal with Covenanters who continued to disobey the law …

For some years, the government wavered between persecuting Covenanters as outlaws, and attempting to reach a compromise which would suit both the government and the Covenanters.

In 1669, the government tried to put an end to conventicles by persuading almost 100 outed ministers to accept pardons called **'Indulgences'** from the King and return to their parishes. But many firm Covenanters denounced ministers who accepted this compromise as traitors to the Covenant. Conventicles grew larger, sometimes with thousands present, all armed against attack. They began to look more like armies than religious gatherings.

In alarm, the government introduced harsher laws against conventicles. Landlords allowing such meetings on their land faced heavy fines, and the penalty for preaching at a conventicle was death.

Some Covenanters thought the time had come for action. In 1679, nine armed Covenanters ambushed and gruesomely murdered the Archbishop of St Andrews, James Sharp. The Covenanters considered Sharp a traitor, as he had been a Covenanter but now he encouraged harsh penalties for those who attended conventicles.

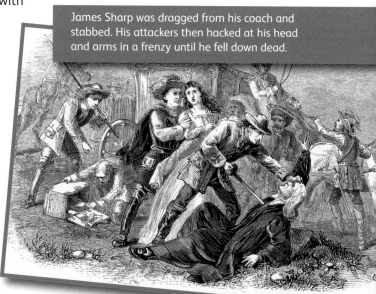

James Sharp was dragged from his coach and stabbed. His attackers then hacked at his head and arms in a frenzy until he fell down dead.

The murderers fled west to join an enormous conventicle taking place at Drumclog. Soldiers tracking them found themselves facing 1500 Covenanters wielding pikes, swords and pitch-forks. Hugely outnumbered and struggling to advance through the boggy ground around Drumclog, the soldiers were forced to retreat to Glasgow, with a mob of Covenanters at their heels.

After their victory at Drumclog, the Covenanters set up camp at Hamilton to wait for more supporters to join them. Here moderate and extremist Covenanters began to disagree over their aims and how these were to be achieved. In the meantime, the government gathered an army. The next time the two sides met, at Bothwell Brig, the 6000-strong Covenanter army was easily defeated by 15,000 government soldiers.

Highland Host

In 1678, the Scottish government sent an army of 3000 Lowlanders and 6000 Highlanders to the south-west to keep order, search out armed rebels and live in the homes of those who would not pay fines, at the expense of the householders. Known as the 'Highland Host', these men swept through south-west Scotland looting and plundering, before they were sent home again. Their brief presence terrorised many, but made other ardent Covenanters all the more determined to fight for their beliefs.

Bothwell Brig

The battle took place on 22 June 1679 around a bridge over the River Clyde in Lanarkshire. The Covenanters held a strong position on one side of the bridge, but once the government troops managed to force their way over, the Covenanters were quickly defeated.

Open prison

There was no prison large enough to house 1400 Covenanter prisoners captured at the Battle of Bothwell Brig. Instead they were confined in open cages in Edinburgh's Greyfriars Churchyard.

Taking the Test

After Bothwell Brig, Covenanters were granted permission to worship at small conventicles in private buildings. For the more extreme among them, this was not enough.

There were no more vast conventicles. The few hundred Covenanters now met in tiny groups like secret societies and known by such names as **'Society Folk'**, the **'Remnant'** or the **'Cameronians'**. These radical Covenanters began to talk of getting rid of kings altogether and setting up a Presbyterian republic.

Such revolutionary ideas made the Covenanters more than just religious rebels. Once again, they were a threat to the King's power. In 1681, the government introduced the **Test Act** which forced officials, government employees and teachers to swear an oath of loyalty to the King and to accept royal authority in all religious and political matters. Anyone who would not 'take the Test' would lose their job and be fined. This would reveal those who were

The Sanquhar Declaration

In 1680, a year to the day after the Battle of Bothwell Brig, 20 armed men rode into the town of Sanquhar in Dumfriesshire, led by the preacher Richard Cameron (1648–1680). They gathered at the Mercat Cross where they sang a psalm and then read out a document declaring war on Charles II. The document was nailed to the cross for all to see. A month later, Cameron was killed in battle at Airds Moss in Ayrshire.

The group known as the **Cameronians** were named after Richard Cameron. They believed that they were the only true Covenanters left in Scotland.

The **Cameronian Regiment** of the British army claimed its roots in the Covenanter Rebellion. Some of the Cameronians offered their services to the government and formed the Cameronian Regiment, which was finally disbanded in 1968.

Covenanters, as their beliefs would not allow them to take the Test.

Government soldiers swept through the country, forcing not just officials but also ordinary people to take the Test.

The authorities were trying to weed out a tiny group of rebels, but their heavy-handed actions only led to the Covenanters going further into hiding. Having little success, the authorities terrorised families and supporters in an attempt to make them betray the rebels. In reaction to such persecution, many people who had been largely law-abiding began to sympathise with the Covenanters.

The Covenanters, meanwhile, grew more extreme, carrying out guerrilla raids, and attacking and murdering soldiers and ministers. They were prepared to die as martyrs for their beliefs.

James VII and II

From 1679 to 1682, Charles II sent his brother and heir, James, Duke of York (1633–1701) to be the Commissioner for Scotland, effectively viceroy in Scotland. People were suspicious of James because he was a Roman Catholic, and thought he might try to impose Catholicism on Scotland, especially after he succeeded his brother to become King James VII in 1685.

'The Killing Time'

There was much bloodshed during the 1680s, and that is why it is often called 'The Killing Time'.

Popular accounts say that when the King's soldiers managed to track down fanatical Covenanters, they tortured them for information about the whereabouts of other wanted men or about what they were plotting to do. Then the Covenanters were executed or sent to be slaves in the colonies.

It is said that when the soldiers could not lay their hands on the Covenanters themselves, they harried and persecuted anyone suspected of sympathising with the Covenanters or of offering them food or shelter. Laws were passed which meant that anyone who refused to deny the most extreme beliefs of the fanatics could be executed immediately without trial. Some people were even executed for stammering while they took an oath denying the Covenant, or simply for carrying a Bible.

The Covenanters and their supporters saw themselves as martyrs dying for their religion. Reports of their deaths say many of them prayed aloud as they were shot, hanged, beheaded or drowned. But there was sense-less killing on the other side of the struggle

John Graham of Claverhouse
known as 'Bluidy Clavers'

The man charged with tracking down the Covenanters was **John Graham of Claverhouse** (1648–1689). The Covenanters blamed him for many atrocities that took place and gave him his nickname. In fact, Claverhouse tried to get people to go back to church and only made an example of the troublemakers. He urged the soldiers to behave moderately, realising that harsh treatment of innocent people would make them support the extremists.

too, as diehard Covenanters were targeting anyone they considered to be a spy or a collaborator for the government.

When the Roman Catholic James VII succeeded to the throne in 1685, the government believed that the underground rebellion might escalate into a revolution. For a time the south-west of Scotland was like a war zone, with soldiers patrolling the countryside, dragging people from their work in the fields to question them. Although persecution of the Covenanters reached a peak at this time, some believe the situation was not as extreme as these accounts record.

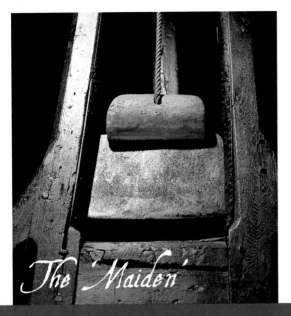

The 'Maiden'

Above: Currently in the National Museum of Scotland in Edinburgh, this device was used to execute the earl of Argyll and many others during 'The Killing Time'. The blade is raised up using a rope. The victim is positioned with their neck on the cross-bar and the heavy blade is dropped, severing the head from the body. As this method of execution was instant, it was considered to be humane.

Below: View across the Solway towards Wigtown.

Inset, far right: A martyr cell in Wigtown; and the 'Drowning Place' (inset, right) is said to represent the stake that the martyrs were tied to. As the sea came in and over their heads, they were left to drown.

In 1685, Margaret MacLachlan, aged 63, and Margaret Wilson, aged 18, were found guilty of supporting extremist Covenanters. As punishment, they were tied to stakes on the Solway shore and drowned by the incoming tide.

Their monument reads: '*Margaret Wilson, aged 18 ... and Margaret MacLachlan, aged 63 ... were drowned by sentence of the Public Authorities in the waters of the Bladnoch near this place on the 11th of May 1685, because they refused to forsake the principles of the Scottish Reformation and to take the government oath, abjuring the right of the people to resist the tyranny of their Rulers.*'

They were not the only ones to suffer in Wigtown that year. William Johnstone, John Milroy and Gilbert Walker were also executed for the same cause.

The Glorious Revolution

After James VII came to the throne in 1685, the persecution of the Covenanters eased …

Most people had started to attend services in the kirks again, either as a result of the fines and harassment, or because they were happy enough with the way the Episcopalian Church of Scotland was being run now. But before long, there were to be more changes to the Church.

Many people in Scotland and England were unhappy that their new king, James VII, was a Roman Catholic – even if the heir to the throne, James's daughter Mary, was a Protestant. It seemed that it was just a matter of time before England and Scotland would be ruled by a Protestant again. However, in 1688 James's wife gave birth to a baby boy. This new heir to the throne was certain to be brought up a Catholic.

Some English politicians decided to invite James's daughter Mary and her Dutch husband, Prince William III of Orange (and grandson of Charles I), to take the throne. William arrived in London at the head of 14,000 men and was proclaimed king, while James fled to France with his wife and baby son, effectively forfeiting the crown. When news of this so-called 'Glorious Revolution' reached Scotland, William and Mary were quickly accepted as the new monarchs.

James VIII & III

James VII's son, who would have been James VIII and III (1688–1766), was considered by many people, and most of the monarchs in Europe, to be the rightful heir to the throne. Although all attempts to restore him to the throne by force were unsuccessful, James lived like a king in Italy, surrounded by exiled courtiers, all at the expense of the Pope.

William would have been happy to leave the Church of Scotland exactly as it was, but most of the bishops and the Episcopalian clergy were still supporters of James, while William's supporters were Presbyterians. In addition, in some parishes the news of William and Mary's accession sparked outbreaks of violence, with mobs driving out the Episcopalian ministers.

William decided it was time to put an end to the religious conflict that had been going on for half a century in Scotland. In 1690, an Act of Parliament re-established the Presbyterian Church of Scotland. Ministers who had been outed since 1661 were restored and a General Assembly was summoned for the first since 1653.

There was no mention of the Covenants which had been at the heart of Scotland's religious turmoil. Most former Covenanters returned to the Church of Scotland, although a few still clung to the Covenants and remained outwith the Church of Scotland.

People slowly began to believe that it was wrong to force others to belong to a Church they could not accept. Eventually, there were no more fines for not attending the parish kirk, and people were permitted to worship however they wished. However, this process took many years.

Although most people accepted William and Mary as the new monarchs, some still supported James. This group were called the **Jacobites**. Their stories are told in two other books in the Scotties series entitled *The Jacobites* and *Scottish Kings and Queens*.

William III & Mary II

To help bring peace to Britain, William III (1650–1702) and Mary II (1662–1694) promised to rule according to the law and to follow the wishes of Parliament. Laws were passed that meant no Catholic could ever come to the throne in the future, and stating that no monarch could raise an army without the consent of Parliament.

The Covenanters – success or failure? What do you think? (See page 40)

A copy of the National Covenant, signed by members of the Scottish Privy Council, 1638. The Covenant was a political and religious manifesto opposing King Charles I's changes to the Scottish church and government.

Glossary

ascending – this book talks about various kings ascending the throne on the death of the previous monarch. This was also called their accession, when they accede to the throne.

chapter – the governing body of a religious community.

civil war – a war among the citizens of one country, rather than between one country and another.

covenant – a legal agreement made (in the case of the Covenanters) between God and the people.

conventicle – a religious meeting of more than five people, outwith the then Episcopalian Church of Scotland.

dean – the head of the governing body of a cathedral.

elder – a leader in the Christian church, usually someone who holds a responsible position in society.

the Engagement – Charles I agreed to confirm the Solemn League and Covenant in the English Parliament, impose Presbyterian church government for a trial three-year period, approve all acts passed by the Scottish Parliament and generally give Scots more power in English government. Crucially, however, he would still not have to sign the Covenant.

Episcopalian – government of a church by bishops.

evangelical – relating to the four Gospels; the belief that humans are sinners, that sinners are freed from guilt by faith alone, that the gospel should be offered free to all, and that the Bible has exclusive authority.

excommunicate – to ban a person from being a member of a Christian Church.

laird – (in Scotland) a person who owns a large estate, land(s), or property.

layman – a person who does not hold an official position in the Church.

liturgy – words, music and actions used in ceremonies in some religions, especially Christianity.

martyr – a person who dies for their religious or other beliefs.

mercenary – a soldier who fights for a foreign country or for money.

Moderator – a person who moderates (regulates) or presides over Presbyterian church courts.

negotiate – to try to reach an agreement or a compromise by discussion.

New Model Army – an independent branch of the army formed in 1645 by the English Parliamentarians during the civil war and disbanded in 1660 when Charles II was restored to the throne.

nobility – the highest class in certain societies, typically comprising people of noble birth and holding hereditary titles, money and land.

Presbyterianism – a form of Protestant church government in which the church is administered locally by the minister with a group of elected elders of equal rank, and regionally by representative courts of ministers and elders.

realm – a kingdom.

royalist – a person who supports the principle of monarchy or a particular monarchy.

the Tables – a rebel parliament consisting of a table each of nobles, lairds, ministers and the burgesses; and an additional one consisting of representatives from each group.

Tolbooth – the Old Tolbooth on the Royal Mile in Edinburgh held official meetings regarding the running of the city. It was also a jail and a place of public execution and torture for criminals. The building was demolished in 1817; the cobblestones of the Heart of Midlothian in front of St Giles' Kirk now mark the site of the old entrance.

treason – the act of betraying someone or something, especially one's country or monarch.

Covenanters' battle re-enactment at Caerlaverock Castle, by the Sealed Knot Society.

ANSWERS

Page 9: Charles I – Charles I introduced the new prayer book because he wanted to make the Church of Scotland more like the Church of England.

Page 13: A united rebellion – The authors of the National Covenant were careful not to sound too revolutionary because they wanted the King to accept their grievances and make changes, not see them as challenging him. They also wanted to make sure as many people as possible signed the Covenant, and a number would have been unwilling to make a direct challenge against authority, even though they were unhappy with the situation.

Page 15: Choosing a venue – The Marquis of Hamilton chose to summon the General Assembly in Glasgow instead of the capital, Edinburgh, because there were less likely to be riots or demonstrations in a small town with only around 5000 inhabitants.

Page 17: Covenanter flag – The flag says: COVENANTS / FOR RELIGION / CROWNE AND / KINGDOMS

Page 20: Mystery object – This is James Graham's powder horn, used to carry gunpowder. It is made of a large cow's horn with a silver base-plate and engraved with his coat of arms.

Page 27: Mystery object – Alexander Peden made a mask of his own face to wear as a disguise.

Page 38: The Covenanters – success or failure? – The Covenanters' fundamental aim was to make the Church of Scotland Presbyterian. This was achieved. However, they did not manage to enforce Presbyterianism throughout Scotland, since other religious groups were now tolerated. Nor did they manage to spread Presbyterianism to other countries in the United Kingdom. They also failed to create a strong, independent government for Scotland.

Facts and activities section

Page ii: Word search – The 20 words related to the Covenanters are highlighted in the box (right).

Page iv: Criss-crossword – (1) Greyfriars; (2) Test; (3) Prophet; (4) Pentland; (5) Jenny; (6) Royalist; (7) Graham; (8) Bishops; (9) Maiden; (10) Solemn

Pages vi–vii: Covenanter's Quiz – (1) b; (2) a=1, b=4, c=2, d=3; (3) b; (4) c; (5) b; (6) d; (7) d; (8) a; (9) b; (10) c; (11) a; (12) b; (13) All eight individuals had some association with the Wars of the Covenant. They are: A = Charles I, B = Marquis of Hamilton, C = William Laud, D = 'Prophet' Peden, E = Alexander Henderson, F = Mary II, G = Charles II, H = Alexander Leslie; (14) d; (15) a; (16) b, c; (17) a and c; (18) c; (19) d; (20) b; (21) a; (22) c; (23) a; (24) d; (25) c; (26) b; (27) d; (28) b; (29) d; (30) c

WEBSITES TO VISIT

BBC history sites:
www.bbc.co.uk/scotland/history/covenanters
www.bbc.co.uk/history/scottishhistory/union/features_union_covenanters.shtml

Blackness Castle (used as a prison for Covenanters):
www.historic-scotland.gov.uk
Click on **'Places to Visit'** to get to **'Find a Place to Visit'**, then type in **'Blackness'**.

Dunnotter Castle ruins (also used as a prison):
www.dunnottercastle.co.uk

Greenhill Covenanters' House:
www.biggarmuseumtrust/home/greenhill-covenanters-house

National Museums Scotland:
www.nms.ac.uk

Scottish Covenanter Memorials Association:
www.covenanter.org.uk/

Full text of the **National Covenant:**
www.constitution.org/eng/conpur023.htm

Full text of the **Solemn League and Covenant:**
www.constitution.org/eng/conpur058.htm